Priyanka Bijlani is a American, Indian, and .   ...heritage and a polyglot (5 languages and counting). She is a graduate of the University of Oxford and a Public Policy professional. Her poetry style and passion for multilingual and multicultural storytelling stems from its power to transcend borders and convey a sense of universality with respect to human emotions and experiences regardless of the parameters in which they emerge.

The Essence of Karak is modern-day compilation of free verse poetry that shares reflections of places and people of inspiration, and encounters that exhibit life's dualities from the perspective of a 21st century millennial woman.

In this collection, Priyanka takes readers on a journey through multiple cultural realms while carrying through the essence of what it takes to be strong or '*karak*'.

The Essence of
كرك
(Karak)

Brewed contemporary poetry

Priyanka R. Bijlani

AUSTIN MACAULEY PUBLISHERS™

LONDON • CAMBRIDGE • NEW YORK • SHARJAH

ISBN – 9789948776062 – (Paperback)
ISBN – 9789948776055– (E-Book)

Application Number: MC-10-01-0743661
Age Classification: E

Printer Name: iPrint Global Ltd
Printer Address: Witchford, England

First Published 2023
AUSTIN MACAULEY PUBLISHERS FZE
Sharjah Publishing City
P.O Box [519201]
Sharjah, UAE
www.austinmacauley.ae
+971 655 95 202

Part I

الشاي اليوم |

Chai Al Youm (Tea today)

These days they say
"هالزمن مب نفس أيام اول"
not like the olden days they chime
as the clocks propel time

but we beg to differ
the leaves remain preserved,
ready to brew –
and will brew – until it simmers
producing strong *karak* flavors and aromas
that exude
the history and heritage
that run through our veins
but that can always be blended, poured –
and sipped again

Future of Dunes

The dunes swept from below
lusting to leap,
lusting to thrust,
lusting to breakthrough

and it rose –
like the power of the sun
that infuses the universe
with the same power,
shedding light on the future

calligraphy embossed structures
erected
between towers of thoughts

that drove visions –
through the region,
through the silk trade roads,
and the pathways of the world lit up

and the sand dunes continue to rise

أمنـا | Our Mother

The tears and sweat behind a push of love
that permeates life all around

did you see what she did?

a gentle stroke,
lifted a nation

Golden Generation

The abras docked by the souq
where he lay low
under the hard sun
against the glistening glare of gold
not knowing where to go

his daughter
starry and bright-eyed
led a pathway
where impossible
was –
but now, just not possible

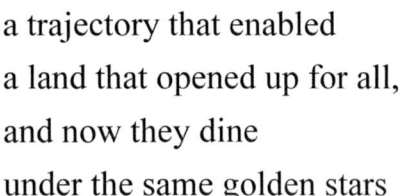

a trajectory that enabled
a land that opened up for all,
and now they dine
under the same golden stars

From the Same Fabric

She crossed paths
they crossed again,
and again, fusing –

donning an abaya, a kimono, and a saree,

encircled around a مجلس (*majlis*)
thoughts that provoked,
as elaborate as the cutwork and embellishments
that they adorned on their garments

and colors bled through the very
structures and traditions
and social fabric
that keep us all grounded,
distinct,
but always –
united

Hint of بخور (*bukhoor*)

The building blocks
that hold the very
essence of family,
connection,
and tradition together

fumigating –
with the concoctions of roses and
woven threads of saffron
infusing realms of life
that celebrates love
and –
that keeps evil at bay
and –
that welcomes you to stay

Reminiscing the بقالة
(*Baqala* – traditional
Arab grocery store)

Browse and click,
share and zoom,
instant gratification looms

in the process,
we have lost the sense –
the sense to touch
the sense to smell
the sense to take a sneaky bite
and to consume the environment and space –

in which we crossed paths,
 in which we opened our eyes,
with the opportunity to –
to peer into,
and to appreciate others' lives

A Balancing Act

Balance in her touch, and his
in her thoughts, and his
in her words, and his
in her actions, and his
in her leadership, and his

and when together we rise
we can reach new highs

نخلات | *Nakhlat*
Your Neighbourhood Palm Trees

The palm trees brought a sense –

of familiarity,
and calmness,
to every street and regional corner

of identity,
and solidity,
to every beach and desert border

that could withstand,
any force of nature –
always standing
and resilient in stature

شجرة الغاف | Ghaf Tree

Resilient and stoic
standing tall –
in the face of gusting shamal winds,
and against the harsh sands

planted to extend an olive branch,
and to stabilize soil

نصيب | *Nasib*

He tried his hardest
but couldn't pluck the date
that orange-chestnut beast
that stood between him and fate

every year,
every season,
changing color,
as he grew inches taller

although physically closer,
was never in reach,
but everyone told him
not to worry, and preached

but when life turned a page
and time aligned
he was granted with all,
all that he needed to fly

أم لؤلؤة | Mother of Pearl

Woven baskets
that rested at shore

and at the helm, were maritime divers
who waited aboard

at dawn they hooked
they dove off the dhows,

and soaked
then basked by the troves of glistening ivory pearls

20

Cords

Her braids wove together – reflecting,
curated elements of her heritage and culture,
leaving some parts behind

she pieced together memories where
storytelling, was the glue that kept her identity well
and alive

from one daughter to another
these were the intergenerational cords
that were never to snap or falter

Global Traces

As her flight descended
the seatbelt sign went off
she paused and looked down
and then smiled and looked out
knowing that her trail of sand and soil
on the heel of her red-soled imported shoes
had followed her home

and would always follow her home
regardless of how far she dreamed to go

Accelerated Journeys

Up and down
between the capital and desert
daily,
the same route
the same pathway
the same guidance
and to all, this was mundane

to her, it was a path of freedom
where, no one – could keep her away

each time she hit the pedal
and stepped on that metal
her mind accelerated to a world of endless
possibilities –
soaring to find new opportunities

Mother Tongues

It is okay to laugh in a dialect
and to cry in another

to share in a language
and to conceal in another

to switch codes
and then to revert

it is okay to embody and infuse
every dimension of yourself
without a dither,
sans hesitation

Bridge

A portal to a new land
of heritage and culture
that seemingly was distinct
but looking closer
blended our values and beliefs,
your aspirations and yearnings
that were never left behind

so let us not run away
but propel forward

Part II

A Small Wonder

Her sleeves rolled up
and a ribbon that lifted her pony
high enough to notice at crossroads,
and at peaks

where she blinked twice,
and had the world at her feet

Salty Water

Salt and water

can heal a wound
but can't suppress the pain

unlike tears
that can leave a reminiscent stain

Bloom Baby, Bloom

They told me to bloom,
but decided where I would be planted.

A Love Concoction

Separating head from heart
like water from oil

until she found joy
then she immersed and
was emulsified

Rooted Love

Rooted
with vines
that grew intertwined,
remaining grounded –
and could stand the test of time

Building a House

It is not ceilings that need be broken

but foundations that need mending
and pillars that need reinforcement

A Daughter is Forever

The same house of three
now two, stood outside
by the bonsai tree, they planted as three

waving as their daughter's henna started to fade
along with her presence they would dearly miss

she hopped into the car
holding onto a bouquet and a newly minted ring
only to turn around
pick up the phone
and give them three rings

Mirror Mirror | Metamorphosis

Every time she winced
in hesitation
she saw a new reflection

what others critiqued as change,
was her blossoming progression

what others questioned as identity,
was a trajectory of her evolution

what others could not digest
her inner mirror revealed –
it was only her impression

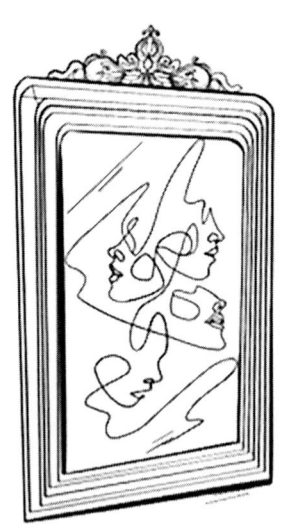

Presence

The needle continued to tick
against her beating heart,
deep breaths, and
sweaty palms

all that was required, however,
which she did not realize
was her presence
in the present

Seismic Waves

Tectonic plates shifting,
systems overturning,
people displacing,
ecosystems replacing

and there under her hood,
in the stillness of the woods,
she stood –
seeking solace
on the axis of multidimensional possibilities

for what was high frequency –
now faded into white noise

Passing on the Dotted Lines

Following the marked traces
she whimsically drew along dotted lines,
uncovering the limits within and
color beyond the parameters,

with each determined stroke –
a new pathway awoke

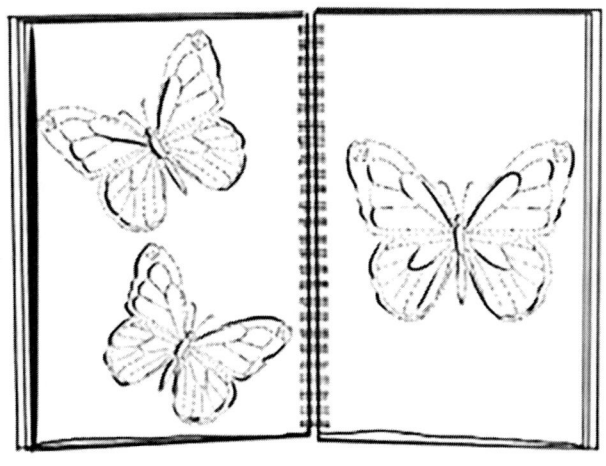

Give and Take

To mend the torn
to heal the bruised
to soothe the hurt
to carry the weight
both you and I and
she and he,
we all, –
share the same –

longing to find solace,
amidst sorrow,
longing to find calm,
amidst chaos.

different cycles,
one lifetime

we give and take,
and at every peak,
and at every trough,

we remain human

Catching Feelings

Her words could leave a stain,
as dark as freshly ground كحل (kohl)

her stares and feelings could seep,
as deep as an overnight brew

her love though –
so scattered
like harvesting saffron strands

رحلتي | My Trip

A trip through four continents that brought me back
home
where I belong,
thank you for coming along,
a journey this long
that I hope to prolong